D0435607

The Secrets of Joy

The Secrets of JOY

A Treasury of Wisdom

RUNNING PRESS
PHILADELPHIA · LONDON

Canadian representatives: General Publishing Co., Ltd.,
30 Lesmill Road, Don Mills, Ontario M3B 2T6.

Library of Congress Cataloging-in-Publication Number
94–67772

ISBN 1–56138–516–6

This book may be ordered from the publisher. Please add
$1.00 for postage and handling. *But try your bookstore first!*
Running Press Book Publishers
125 South Twenty-second Street
Philadelphia, Pennsylvania 19103–4399

CONTENTS

INTRODUCTION

So many experiences can inspire in us that exquisite sense of well-being we identify as joy: a kind word from a casual acquaintance or an embrace from a lover, an accomplishment recognized by colleagues or the quiet realization of a personal goal, an evening of euphoric celebration or merely a moment of peace spent indulging in one of life's simple pleasures.

The opportunities to be joyful abound,

yet we are sometimes so preoccupied
with seeking after happiness that we fail to
recognize it and neglect to savor it when it
enters our lives. Our desire to discover an
enduring state of peace and happiness keeps
us looking beyond the present and blinds
us to the smaller occasions that can be
so gratifying.

The voices in this book—those of
writers, artists, thinkers, and leaders from
throughout the centuries—remind us that we
must always keep our hearts open to
unexpected sources of joy, and offer us

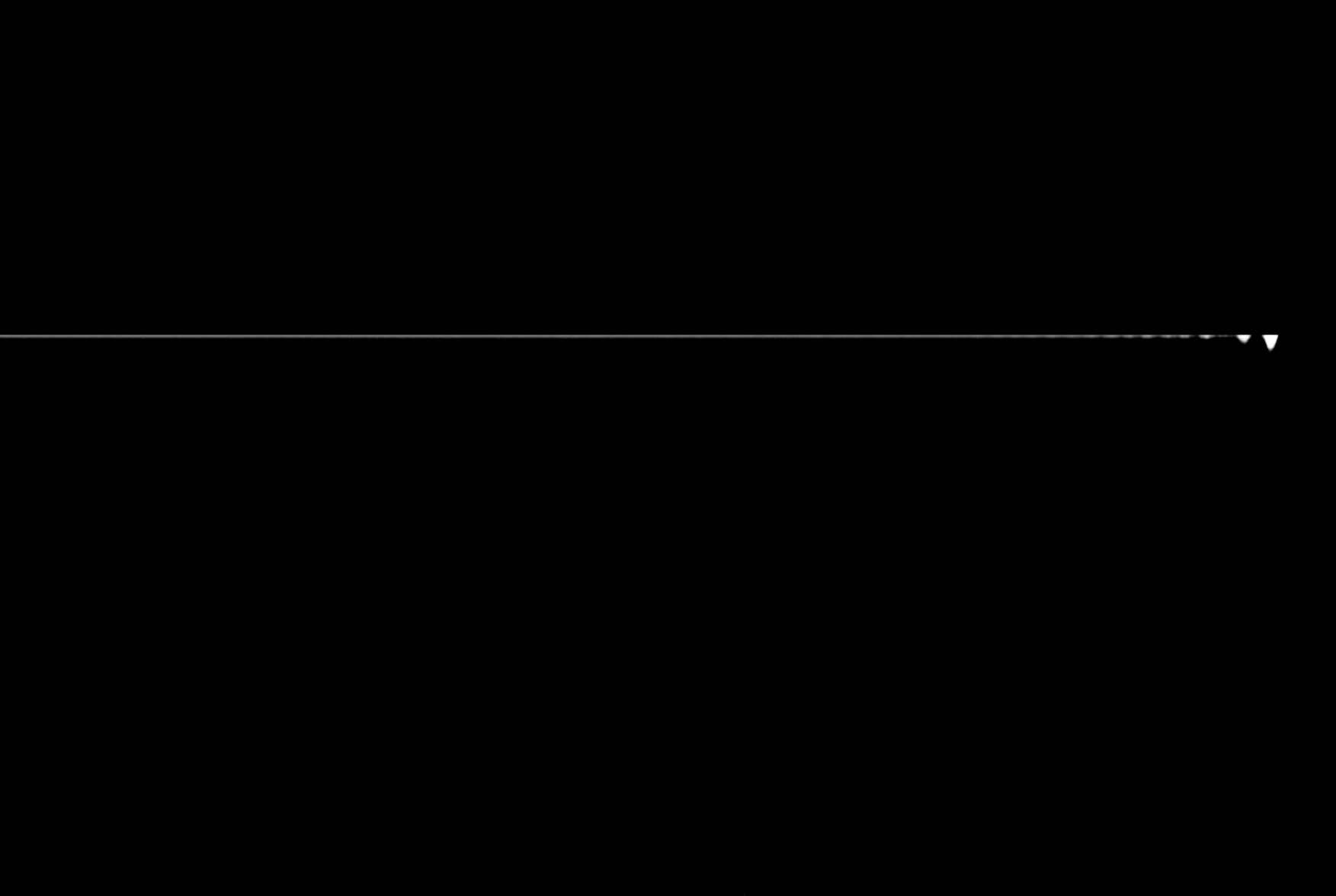

insights to the secrets of prolonging its experience. The wisdom of their words gives pause for thought and provides a deeper appreciation of the delights we often over-look. There is no single key to happiness, they tell us. Rather, we must learn to rejoice in the infinite variety of pleasures life can bring.

Treasure this book as one of those pleasures. Delight in the simple truths it contains. Above all, share the gladness in its pages with others in your life. For joy, contagious as a smile, demands to be spread.

SEEKING HAPPINESS

*J*oy has no cost.

Marianne Williamson (b. 1953)
American writer

*J*oy is a free, unrestrained passion.

Eileen Stukane
20th-century American journalist
and writer

*J*oy is a net of love by which
you can catch souls. . . . A joyful
heart is the inevitable result of a
heart burning with love.

Mother Teresa (b. 1910)
Albanian missionary

One imagines joy as a flame. Like all flames it needs oxygen, some life force, a combustible material, a significant activity, and then the white heat of profound effort or activity leading ultimately to inner satisfaction, if not ebullience.

Thomas J. Cottle (b. 1937)
American psychologist

Happiness is a how, not a what; a talent, not an object.

Hermann Hesse (1877–1962)
German writer

*H*ow many joys are crushed underfoot because people look up at the sky and disregard what is at their feet.

attributed to the mother of Johann Wolfgang von Goethe (1749–1832) German poet

When one door of happiness closes, another opens; but often we look so long at the closed door that we do not see the one which has been opened for us.

Helen Keller (1880–1968)
American writer and lecturer

*H*appiness is not a goal,
it is a by-product.

Eleanor Roosevelt (1884–1962)
American writer and First Lady

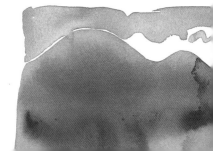

The foolish man seeks
happiness in the distance;
The wise grows it under his feet.

James Oppenheim (1882–1932)
American poet

Action may not always bring happiness; but there is no happiness without action.

Benjamin Disraeli (1804–1881)
English politician

"*If* thou wouldst know contentment, let thy deeds be few," said the sage. Better still, limit them strictly to such as are essential, and to such as in a social being reason demands, and as it demands. This brings the contentment that comes of doing a few things and doing them well.

Marcus Aurelius (121–180)
Roman emperor and philosopher

*T*he happiest person is the person who thinks the most interesting thoughts.

Timothy Dwight (1828–1916)
American minister and professor

*H*appiness is a mystery, like religion, and should never be rationalized.

G.K. Chesterton (1874–1936)
British writer

There are two things to aim at in life: first, to get what you want; and, after that, to enjoy it. Only the wisest of mankind achieve the second.

Logan Pearsall Smith (1865–1946)
American essayist

*F*rom contentment with little comes happiness.

African proverb

*H*appiness is not having
what you want, but wanting
what you have.

Hyman Judah Schachtel (1907–1990)
American rabbi and writer

I'm fulfilled in what I do. . . .
I never thought that a lot of
money or fine clothes—the
finer things of life—would
make you happy. My concept
of happiness is to be fulfilled
in a spiritual sense.

Coretta Scott King (b. 1927)
American civil rights leader

Cultivate more joy by arranging your life so that more joy will be likely.

Georgia Witkin (b. 1943)
American professor of psychiatry

*W*ell-being is attained by little and little, and nevertheless it is no little thing itself.

Zeno of Citium (c. 335–c. 263 B.C.)
Greek philosopher

*I*t is not easy to find happiness
in ourselves, and it is not
possible to find it elsewhere.

Agnes Repplier (1855–1950)
American writer

*H*appiness depends more on how life strikes you than on what happens.

Andy Rooney (b. 1919)
American broadcaster and writer

*T*he secret of happiness is not
in doing what one likes, but in
liking what one has to do.

James M. Barrie (1860–1937)
Scottish novelist and dramatist

There is no duty we so much underrate as the duty of being happy.

Robert Louis Stevenson (1850–1894)
Scottish writer

*H*appiness is like those palaces in fairy tales whose gates are guarded by dragons: we must fight in order to conquer it.

Alexandre Dumas (1824–1895)
French playwright and novelist

*H*appiness is not a horse, you cannot harness it.

Russian proverb

*H*appiness ain't a *thing in itself*—
it's only a *contrast* with something
that ain't pleasant. . . . And so, as
soon as the novelty is over and
the force of the contrast dulled,
it ain't happiness any longer, and
you have to get something fresh.

Mark Twain (1835–1910)
American writer

Ask yourself whether you are happy, and you cease to be so.

John Stuart Mill (1806–1873)
English philosopher

*T*he search for happiness is
one of the chief sources
of unhappiness.

Eric Hoffer (1902–1983)
American philosopher

I sometimes wonder whether all pleasures are not substitutes for Joy.

C.S. Lewis (1898–1963)
British writer and theologian

*T*he greatest happiness you can have is knowing that you do not necessarily require happiness.

William Saroyan (1908–1981)
American writer

. . . joy runs deeper than despair.

Corrie ten Boom
20th-century Dutch evangelist

One joy scatters a hundred griefs.

Chinese proverb

*F*or every minute you are angry
you lose sixty seconds of
happiness.

Ralph Waldo Emerson (1803–1882)
American essayist and poet

*H*appiness makes up in height
what it lacks in length.

Robert Frost (1874–1963)
American poet

*B*ut a lifetime of happiness!
No man alive could bear it:
it would be hell on earth.

George Bernard Shaw (1856–1950)
British playwright and critic

*H*e who binds to himself a joy
Does the winged life destroy;
But he who kisses the joy
    as it flies
Lives in Eternity's sunrise.

William Blake (1757–1827)
English poet

*T*here is only one way to happiness and that is to cease worrying about things which are beyond the power of our will.

Epictetus (c. 55-c. 135)
Greek philosopher

*W*hat we call the secret of happiness is no more a secret than our willingness to choose life.

Leo Buscaglia (b. 1924)
American professor and writer

SIMPLE PLEASURES

Our brightest blazes of gladness are commonly kindled by unexpected sparks.

Samuel Johnson (1709–1784)
English writer

. . . a leaf fluttered in through
the window this morning, as if
supported by the rays of the
sun, a bird settled on the fire
escape, joy in the task of
coffee, joy accompanied
me as I walked. . . .

Anaïs Nin (1903–1977)
French-born American writer

I have told you of the Spaniard
who always put on his spectacles
when about to eat cherries, that
they might look bigger and
more tempting. In like manner
I make the most of my
enjoyments; and though I do

not cast my cares away, I
pack them in as little compass
as I can, and carry them as
conveniently as I can for myself,
and never let them annoy others.

Robert Southey (1774–1843)
English poet

A hot bath! I cry, as I sit down in it; and again, as I lie flat, a hot bath! How exquisite a vespertine pleasure, how luxurious, fervid and flagrant a consolation for the rigours, the austerities, the renunciations of the day.

Rose Macaulay (1881–1958)
British writer

Give me books, fruit, French
wine and fine weather and a
little music out of doors, played
by someone I do not know.

John Keats (1795–1821)
English poet

. . . interests, whether in writing history, breeding carrier pigeons, speculating in stocks and shares, designing aircraft, playing the piano, or gardening, play a greater part in the economy of human happiness than modern psycho-analysts and their followers allow.

Anthony Storr (b. 1920)
English writer and psychotherapist

*I*n things pertaining to
enthusiasm, no man is sane
who does not know how to be
insane on proper occasions.

Henry Ward Beecher (1813–1887)
American clergyman, editor, and writer

What is a demanding pleasure?
A pleasure that demands the
use of one's mind; not in the
sense of problem solving,
but in the sense of exercising
discrimination, judgement,
awareness.

Ayn Rand (1905–1982)
American writer

*I*t appears to me that it is the special province of music to move the heart.

Karl Philipp Emanuel Bach
(1714–1788)
German composer

Scratching is one of nature's sweetest gratifications, and the nearest at hand.

Michel de Montaigne (1533–1592)
French essayist

*F*or one mother, joy is the quiet pleasure found in gently rubbing shampoo into her young child's hair. For another woman it's taking a long walk alone, while for yet another it's reveling in a much-anticipated vacation.

Eileen Stukane
20th-century American journalist
and writer

*W*hen everything is all very green, when winter is over and everything is warm and the sun is coming north, when the birds holler *witwitwit*, the people begin to ask,

"Why can't we play a little?"
Then they send news to their
close neighbors that they are
going to have a dance. . . .

Jeff Jones
20th-century Native American
(Nomlaki) speaker

73

In my country, aged people have the right to live with the younger people. It is the grandparents who tell fairy tales to the children. When they get old, their skin is cold and wrinkled, and it is a great joy for them to hold their grandchild, so warm and tender.

Thich Nhat Hanh (b. 1926)
Vietnamese Zen master, writer,
and peace activist

*W*hat a blessing is the childish
nature which clothes dull
surroundings in fancy dress
and drives dull cares away.
The sand pile where we played
after the red sun went down was
transformed into moats and
castles with just as much
enjoyment as if the land, like
Canaan, had been flowing with
milk and honey.

Anonymous 19th-century female pioneer

*T*o see a World in a Grain
  of Sand
And a Heaven in a Wild Flower
Hold Infinity in the palm of
  your hand
And Eternity in an hour . . .

William Blake (1757–1827)
English poet

I could hear crickets singing and frogs croaking and all the other gentle night sounds of the country. I felt as though I were in another more immense, never-ending world, and wished I could keep riding forever to the ends of the earth.

Yoshiko Uchida (1921–1992)
Japanese-American writer

*J*oking is undignified; that is why it is so good for one's soul.

G.K. Chesterton (1874–1936)
British writer

*T*hinking a smile all the time
will keep your face youthful.

Frank Gelett Burgess (1866–1951)
American humorist and illustrator

*W*rinkles should merely indicate
where smiles have been.

Mark Twain (1835–1910)
American writer

Giving Joy

Scatter joy.

Ralph Waldo Emerson (1803–1882)
American essayist and poet

All love is sweet,
Given or returned. Common as
    light is love,
And its familiar voice wearies
    not ever. . . .
They who inspire it most are
    fortunate,
As I am now; but those who feel
    it most
Are happier still.

Percy Bysshe Shelly (1792–1822)
English poet

The supreme happiness
of life is the conviction that
we are loved.

Victor Hugo (1802–1885)
French novelist

All who joy would win
Must share it,—Happiness was
    born a Twin.

George Gordon, Lord Byron
(1788–1824)
English poet

Let no one ever come to you
without leaving better and
happier. Be the living expression
of God's kindness; kindness in
your face, kindness in your eyes,
kindness in your smile.

Mother Teresa (b. 1910)
Albanian missionary

Warm weather fosters growth; cold weather destroys it. Thus a man with an unsympathetic temperament has scant joy; but a man with a warm and friendly heart has overflowing blessings, and his beneficence will extend to posterity.

Hung Tzu-ch'eng (c. 1600)
Chinese Zen Buddhist monk

*H*appiness is a matter of one's most ordinary everyday mode of consciousness being busy and lively and unconcerned with self. To be damned is for one's ordinary everyday mode of consciousness to be unremitting agonising preoccupation with self.

Iris Murdoch (b. 1919)
British novelist

If I thought that a word
   of mine
     Perhaps unkind and untrue,
Would leave its trace on a loved
   one's face,
     I'd never speak it—
       Would you?

If I thought that a smile of
    mine
    Might linger the whole day
    through
And lighten some heart with a
    heavier part,
    I'd not withhold it—
        Would you?

Anonymous

*H*appiness is perfume, you can't pour it on somebody else without getting a few drops on yourself.

James Van DerZee (1886–1983)
American photographer

"Who be she?" he says. And even though it be only a passing thought and three words, I'm a flower that knows the sun.

Mary Webb (1881–1927)
British writer and poet

A principal fruit of friendship is the ease and discharge of the fulness and swellings of the heart, which passions of all kinds do cause and induce.

Francis Bacon (1561–1626)
English philosopher

Always serve too much hot fudge sauce on hot fudge sundaes. It makes people overjoyed, and puts them in your debt.

Judith Olney
20th-century
American chef

As in filling a vessel drop by drop, there is at last a drop which makes it run over; so in a series of kindnesses there is at last one which makes the heart run over.

James Boswell (1740–1795)
Scottish lawyer and biographer

My creed is that:
Happiness is the only good.
The place to be happy is here.
The time to be happy is now.
The way to be happy is to make others so.

Robert G. Ingersoll (1833–1899)
American lawyer and orator

*L*et us be grateful to people
who make us happy; they are the
charming gardeners who make
our souls blossom.

Marcel Proust (1871–1922)
French novelist

THE
JOYFUL

We are happy when for everything inside us there is a corresponding something outside us.

William Butler Yeats (1865–1939)
Irish poet and playwright

My life has no purpose, no direction, no aim, no meaning, and yet I'm happy. I can't figure it out. What am I doing right?

Charles M. Schulz (b. 1922)
American cartoonist

What we feel matters much
more than what we know.

George Moore (1852–1933)
Irish writer

*H*appiness was not made to be boasted, but enjoyed. Therefore tho' others count me miserable, I will not believe them if I know and feel myself to be happy. . . .

Thomas Traherne (1636–1674)
English poet and clergyman

*W*e are made happy when reason can discover no occasion for it. The memory of some past moments is more persuasive than the experience of present ones. There have been visions of such breadth and brightness that these motes were invisible in their light.

Henry David Thoreau (1817–1862)
American writer and philosopher

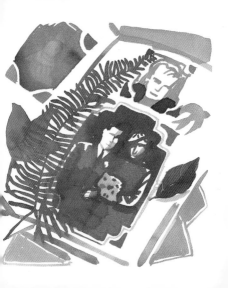

Unexpected joy is always so
keen that . . . it seems to hold
enough to reconcile one to
the inevitable.

Jessie B. Fremont (1824–1902)
American writer and activist

I have found that most people are about as happy as they make up their minds to be.

Abraham Lincoln (1809–1865)
Sixteenth President of the
United States

A man is happy so long
as he chooses to be happy and
nothing can stop him.

Alexander Solzhenitsyn (b. 1918)
Russian writer

*T*here are some people who have the quality of richness and joy in them and they communicate it to everything they touch. It is first of all a physical quality; then it is a quality of the spirit.

Thomas Wolfe (1900–1938)
American novelist

Walking, I am listening to a deeper way. Suddenly all my ancestors are behind me. Be still, they say. Watch and listen. You are the result of the love of thousands.

Linda Hogan (b. 1947)
Native American writer

For many children, joy comes as the result of mining something unique and wondrous about themselves from some inner shaft.

Thomas J. Cottle (b. 1937)
American psychologist

*T*he happiest moments of my life have been the few which I have passed at home in the bosom of my family.

Thomas Jefferson (1743–1826)
Third President of the United States

. . . there came to me, I cannot tell whence, a most powerful sweetness that had never come to me afore. It was not religious, like the goodness of a text heard at a preaching. It was beyond that.

Mary Webb (1881–1927)
British writer and poet

The sobs and tears of joy he
had not foreseen rose with such
force within him that his whole
body shook and for a long time
prevented him from speaking.

Falling on his knees by her
bed, he held his wife's hand to
his lips and kissed it, and her
hand responded to his kisses

with a weak movement of fingers. Meanwhile, at the foot of the bed, in the midwife's expert hands, like the flame of a lamp, flickered the life of a human being who had never existed before. . . .

Leo Tolstoy (1828–1910)
Russian writer

'Tis so much joy! 'Tis so
    much joy!
If I should fail, what poverty!
And yet, as poor as I
Have ventured all upon a throw;
Have gained! Yes! Hesitated so
This side the victory!

Emily Dickinson (1830–1886)
American poet

Hope springs eternal in the
human breast:
Man never is, but always to
be blest.

Alexander Pope (1688–1744)
English poet

*W*hat a wonderful life I've had!
I only wish I'd realized it sooner.

Colette (1873–1954)
French writer

. . . with an eye made quiet by
    the power
Of harmony, and the deep
    power of joy,
We see into the life of things.

William Wordsworth (1770–1850)
English poet

*T*he most evident token
and apparent sign of true
wisdom is a constant and
unconstrained rejoicing.

Michel de Montaigne (1533–1592)
French essayist

May you live all the days of your life.

Jonathan Swift (1667–1745)
English poet

This book has been bound using handcraft methods, and is
Smyth-sewn to ensure durability.

The dust jacket was designed by Toby Schmidt
and illustrated by Meilo So.

The interior was designed by Nancy Loggins Gonzalez
and illustrated by Melio So.

The text was set in MT Centaur by Deborah Joy Lugar.